Precipitous Life

a true story of sudden grief

Tom Pelly

For Elise – my touchstone

"So we drove on toward death through

the cooling twilight"

F. Scott Fitzgerald, The Great Gatsby

One

My brother died suddenly and unexpectedly, a few days after Christmas. It was a total shock: life changing, dramatic, heart-wrenching shock.

A total aberration, of course.

We'd been together with my parents for the holidays. Naturally, that pre-Covid time was filled with festive hot fugs in the kitchen, hugs and close proximity. Matt, the second son, was on great family form.

Like her five children, my Mum had also grown up in Wake House. Our deep-rooted family home, the fortunate old vicarage, next to the church in the heart of a tiny village. All so familiar. All strong, solid, and safe. All calm, predictable and reassuringly stable.

We ended our festivities without drama, leaving the happily-backwater countryside of rural Wiltshire to return to Bristol and work. We left bathed in the cold Thursday sunshine, crisp frost, and love.

I hear the news that Saturday. I've only made it as far as sitting on the edge of the bed, morning tea yet to motivate me.

Wake House ring. They never call early.

How do you know something is wrong? Perhaps just the clarity of retrospect, though that subtle feeling of dread? It is here, in that Hello.

"Matt's been found at the bottom of the church tower, he's fallen. It doesn't look good. He's being flown to the hospital in Southampton." He can hardly get his words out.

As the most senior sibling-in-residence, Adam, number three, is urgently delegated to ring me and the youngest, my sister Claire, back in London on night shifts. His fear and breathlessness palpable. Dad and Chris, my youngest brother, are still with the ambulance crew and police, now in blue-lit panic.

Does he say any more? I don't know. Time doesn't exactly stand still, though it etches indelibly. The record-button presses down hard.

Oddly, I finish cutting my nails before I react. It somehow seems important to complete the task. The slow metallic click of the clipper subconsciously linking itself in my brain with an embedded feeling of fear.

A dense blanket of cloying, acrid smoke envelopes me. Knocks me out.

I cry, head in hands. The news wrenches sobs and renders total emptiness. The retreat to bed is primal.

Two

We went to pick teasels, to spray-paint silver and gold. They'll hang in the hall. Bright, sharp, dramatic decorations. Spikey Christmas frivolity. A tradition my wife Elise loves to uphold.

They'd sit with a green-black background of smooth ivy. Winter colours. Our holly never did have those dramatic red berries of the classic Yuletide look, though perfection was not important. The process is what counted.

It was nippy. A proper December day, blustery, dove-grey and soulful. Good to be out, once you'd made it past the protection of the door.

We set off when everyone was ready. A mandatory march, to counter the cooped up, indoor feeling that creates arguments. A worthy walk with a purpose, to collect supplies in those busy days leading up to Christmas Eve.

Waiting for the laggards and motivated by the freezing air, a game broke out. Three generations of brief yet happy tag. The grandparents stood as observing pillars, immovable, yet somehow integral to the action. My three kids and their cousins loved the drama of their uncles and aunts being unusually animated for a few moments, as they ran and roared at them with joy over the gravel. Sudden changes of direction left temporary scars in the ground as the stones bunched up underfoot. Squeaks of excitement.

Matt was still pulling on his boots and missing out on the action. He arrived outside smiling benignly at the frisson, unknowingly sending the signal to cease the game and depart.

Once up the road, we settled into uncoordinated groups as the walk sets off round the field. Clusters of chat, jokes, and banal practicality. As the eldest, my role the boring pragmatist, reliable and predictable.

"Have you got a lead for the dog, Tom?"

We meandered on our familiar route. A normal Pelly family event. Prosaic and mundane; yet important. A well understood routine.

Matt wore his favourite grey woollen hat, half baseball, half flat. Part of the ritual. He's always had a hat, stemming from an early desire to cover his blond childhood curls that he hated and everyone else commented on. *Why do grown-ups do that?!*

His hair was brown and short, with no residual evidence of curls. The hat perhaps now needed to cover more than a little hairline recession. There was no sense of danger. No flicker of what was about to happen.

Teasel corner was in the far reach of the walk. Clusters of brown pointy drama in amongst the weather-battered wet grass. A grown-up job to cut them, despite enthusiastic efforts against this advice.

"They're too spikey, Mum!", complained JoJo, my youngest who's seven, "Can I use the sprayer when we get home?"

We arrived back in the dusk, invigorated and expecting tea. Someone was already layering newspaper over the kitchen table. The spray-can's ball-bearing jumping up and down in gleeful anticipation.

Three

I can hardly walk to the car. The tears have gone, replaced by a bright white flash-gun blindness.

Elise makes rapid plans with her parents, luckily staying for a few days, sensing the loving priority to tell the children we must go immediately. Their open mouths, tears, and trauma to be dealt with later.

She drives the two hours to Southampton, and I sit mute and unmoving, staring out of the passenger window, a distant bystander.

Flattened. A motorway coke can, crushed under an endless torrent of slow lane lorries.

I don't dare ring on the journey for an update. Afraid of what I might find.

My thoughts batter me:

Who knows what we'll find? Him smiling in A&E, a super-lucky escape?

Perhaps he's dead. Why haven't they told us yet? Can I dream of some hope?

No, quickly replaced in my mind by the likelihood of tragedy. I can't count on hope.

How strange this new fork in the road. How alien and grisly.

We arrive at the hospital, and my sister Claire runs out to find us in the car park. Grabs us, her face filled with horror and streaming eyes, expressions mirrored. My feelings of ghastly emptiness now overflowing with fearful anticipation, all pent up.

The relatives' room at A&E is filled with my family. There is a thick unpleasant atmosphere, a nasty syrupy smell. So happily playing tag now reduced to hugs and grim silence. One player missing.

Yet having hurried with such purpose, we are then just waiting. Worrying and waiting.

Waiting.

Mum the hardest to console. She is still stunned like a floating fish. Trapped in unspeaking robotic blankness.

Waiting.

The urgency has evaporated. The air sucked out.

Four

We were drinking too much, encouraged by our last night altogether. The dinner chatty, buoyant, and loving. We were teasing and joking in the time-honoured way. Talking boisterously over each other in a way Elise finds tiresome.

It was easy to settle back into old childhood family positions. Me, the bossy elder brother. Matt the comfortable second, a TV director and documentary-maker by trade; full of wit, often barbed (and only since he became more grown up), with a knowing smile of apology if he pushed too far. Adam the middle, the third boy, enjoying jousting for air with his big brothers. Chris, reminded of his parents' failing strength against the weight of children, independent and loud in case he gets forgotten. Claire, fourteen years younger than me, and eight years younger than Chris, the longed-for daughter, spoilt with brothers, though very much not in life.

Our closeness and irritating wind-ups of each other slowly pushed our parents and partners to bed after a delicious Wake House feast. A celebration of family and the end of the holidays together.

It was the early hours, arms round each other, singing Queen songs on a gaudy plastic karaoke machine, a child's present. The sitting room smelt of pine needles and woodsmoke from the fire, that unmistakable scent of Christmas.

It was wonderful: the camaraderie, the siblinghood and the joy of unabandoned singing. It's true that the videos did not prove the quality of vocal talent that I heard at the time, though the happiness was abundantly evident.

Five

We are led to the ITU Consultant. "He's had a very serious brain injury, brought by the Air Ambulance, as you know, there's nothing we can do, would you like to see him?"

Breathless update or was it just my breathless hearing?

The image of him lying there, just a small graze to the forehead, will be with me forever.

I'd assumed that I would always be immune to the hospital environment; as a doctor, I had been there so many times before. The pervasive smell, the white brightness, the sterile bleeps. The clinical hit so familiar.

What is not familiar is seeing that old friend of mine, my brother, on his deathbed. The plastic breathing tube shoved brutally down his throat.

He looks as if he might wake up too, not very injured. Panic sets in.

GET UP MATT! For pity's sake, we've got to get out of here! GET UP!

He does not move.

We stroke his hair, kiss him, curse him, cry at him and with each other.

How long are we there? Half an hour, an hour, I don't know; not very long.

His usual wit and cutting jibes have been cruelly bashed from him. Like a fly, swatted, his spirit and soul gone in an instant, leaving a stale curled-up corpse.

He's evaporated, leaving us all behind in our despair, our distress, our disbelief.

How can he die? This is not the way it should be, not the natural order of things. He is fit and healthy and so full of life! How can this be?

And then they come to tell us, bluntly yet kindly, that it is time.

We stay out of sight for the final event. That hateful tube removed; the machines carefully turned off.

Once he died, we leave the ITU and set off outside into a forever changed world.

A perfunctory parting, the only thing to do. Like leaving the cinema late on a murky night; best to scurry home. Retreat. Nothing else to do.

Six

My first and last memories of Matt contain a gash to his head. Pale and vulnerable.

We were high on a hillside. Overlooking verdant green forest and a river far in the valley below. Our chalk path skirted the pastel cliffs.

We had skipped happily ahead of the group; my parents and their friends. The view became a natural pause, with the opportunity to throw stones in the river, or at least towards it.

It was 1984. An Olympic summer: Los Angeles, I think.

I was eight and so in my mind, quite capable of the discus. I was two years older and so Matt watched in admiration as I spun and spun in athletic TV emulation.

When my self-induced light-headedness had settled, I searched for my stone over the dusty cliff. Awkwardly, it hadn't sailed into a world-record distance, it'd hit my brother, square on the forehead.

He was wan and the immediate surprise had so far prevented tears.

Red blood spattered the dry white path.

Seven

We arrive home and look at someone else's lasagne.
Delivered by some unknown outsider, looking on and
feeling helpless, lovingly wondering what to do, probably
knowing that whatever they did wouldn't register.

I can't get that final image out of my head. Him just lying
in that clean white bed. Flat and dead.

Surprisingly, it doesn't follow that my dread will keep me
awake. A sound night's sleep after such trauma seems
unlikely, though is what happens. I am just so incredibly
drained.

The next morning the recollection of horror is instant.

Opening the curtain the hardest sting, seeing the vicious

church and its stone-cold tower, from where he fell.

Beaming at us, vindictively. It is Sunday.

That persistent image and my mind's whirrings about all

that preceded it will have plenty of chance to eat at me

later, of course.

Sleep in the first few weeks haunted by replaying those

events, over and over.

What was he doing up there⋯?

What was he feeling?

Had we missed the signs?

Silly boy!

Stupid selfish man.

Fucking idiot!

I cannot believe he's gone.

What was he thinking?

Oh my God; THIS HORROR.

And then over and over.

I know, of course, about the seven textbook stages of loss. I don't realize that they'll cycle so rapidly and carelessly around. Spinning and bouncing recklessly into one another.

A tumultuous tumble of thoughts and feelings, unregulated and uncontrolled. Emotional vertigo. It is a deadly whirlpool, sucking me abysswards as the night wears on.

I don't have much denial, yet that hardly insulates me from the rest. Acceptance still a slow worn path. Now like an old jumper that somehow seems to fit better than the others. It seems to know my shape, my smell, the way I move.

Eight

Rosa and I ran. Her training schedule demanded it. Christmas extravagance my motivation.

"Fancy going up the track in the rain, Dad?", my eldest had a quizzically raised eyebrow, inherited from her mother.

"Ha-ha not much but let's go. I think it's stopped actually··· Matt and Henry are going out to play tennis".

We came back, invigorated by the hills, the chill and the rush of blood to our faces.

The match paused on the tennis court as they heard us coming home and turned to tease us as we passed. The thrill of some in-joke. Raucous happy laughing; an intimate moment. They got back to the game.

Rosa grimaced teenagerly at her annoying younger brother.

I heard Matt encouraging, "Go for the killer shot, Henry. I've always lacked that decisive instinct. I just like playing good shots rather than winning."

His ten-year-old nephew lapped up the attention.

Nine

The world has changed and is yet so well worn. Breakfast?
I can't eat. The coffee to slay the caffeine addiction? It
bounces off my insatiable tiredness.

I have a growing, growling, gnawing nausea; my stomach
up in my throat.

The events of the day before have dried my mouth
irreparably. Mute.

The news has spread. The beacons are lit and bring an
immediate response. Cards drop through the door. Meals,
carefully prepared and lovingly packaged, start to pile up
on the side, albeit ignored.

Without warning, a freezer appears in the front porch, fills with food as it becomes evident that there is a rota to feed us; those who would not be bothered to feed themselves. The devoted community swings into full embrace.

There is talk of people coming to the church.

"We haven't arranged a service, though people would like to come and sit - to pay their respects. Do you mind?"

Do I mind?

I can only shake my head. I'm not going where others would be.

The idea of seeing village mourners is too much to contend with on the first day of grief.

As children, the church was where we went every Sunday. It was growing up. Always part of us, though now in a cultural and traditional sense rather than one borne out of any religious duty. My parents were married there: the connection literally generations old.

It's now too where my brother had just died - breaching some promise of God to keep him safe? Perhaps climbing the cold-hearted tower was his own doing, overriding any heavenly protection.

In a bid to start to comprehend, I stumble leaden legged round the church, to see the place. I want to go early, with Elise guiding my arm, to avoid seeing anyone who might be coming to the church. That dryness in my mouth stops me speaking. Why would I want to see anyone else, in this turmoil?

The broken tiles, just two, a modest remnant of the disaster. The grass is flattened, though no other evidence remains. Everything else taken away in that helicopter with my brother. Or lovingly tidied, unseen, by a grim-faced neighbour.

Just then, Paul walks round the corner, in tears. He's come promptly, come too to bear witness. Paul also grew up in the village, an honorary brother. Luckily for me his mouth is also parched, and we communicate our devastation entirely through our hug.

Paul's father appears. Having taken us to school when we grew up, he too knows us and our family intimately. He too crumples. We hug. There is no quenching, no option to speak.

By now, the little lych gate is sheltering another family friend with tear-stained eyes. They look at me sternly, lovingly, caringly, unbelievingly. Envelope me in hugs and move inside the church. More people stand behind them. More old friends, people who knew me when I was growing up.

And having tried to avoid this, and with the rest of my family inside the safety of Wake House kitchen, I am unwittingly the representative of these dark-clad mourners who are looking for a place to show their anguish and to dole out plaintive cries.

The vicar arrives, to this not-a-church service. Now filled, the drums have beaten multitudes of people to the church pews, where from the roof above them only 24 hours earlier, Matt had plummeted pointlessly onto the frozen, iron-hard ground of the churchyard.

Interrupting mid-silence - for this was not a service - the heavy iron latch to the church door lifted accusatorily, and Andrew appears from London. I have no idea how he had heard what'd happened. No idea he was coming. He pushes past and grabs me; no words needed. An age-old friend. A former flat mate of Matt's. An ally, riding in.

The vicar lights a candle. Prays for the church that had been violated by a violent death within its bounds. *"No sanctuary can be here until this balance is restored through prayer."* My fury rises as I realise her primary thoughts were with the building, not my dead brother.

My anger blows over me like baking hot air on a sunny beach, I am oblivious to everything else, except that unslakable dryness in the mouth.

Ten

The odd post-Christmas lull. Endless eating, drinking, TV, games. An unusually timeless existence.

JoJo and Matt had pulled out her Lego, a new toy. It's fun, though they did it in the background. True, the instructions were ticked off as they should have been, sequentially and logically, though this wasn't the amusement. The titters and simple chat drew me down the hallway to investigate.

They were just enjoying each other's radiant company, uncle and niece. That contentment of privilege, space, time, plenty. It was a rare moment.

Self-absorbed and bathing in each other's sunlight, the mutual effect was one to cherish.

I watched from the side-lines, and they barely looked up. Luckily, they were too engaged to be changed by a spectator.

They'd invented a giggling game. The first to burst out laughing was the loser, with the other doing strange fake chortling to try to knock over their opponent's emotional goblet.

Eleven

Who knows what happens after this? Not me. There is searing angst and horror. All being reflected in my beloved family. My tears trigger theirs, and theirs mine. We stagger around in a fugue, a trance, punch-drunk. Detached yet horribly together. Hollowed out.

The trauma of seeing my family grieving adds to the sharp pungent memory of my brother. Processing the daily shock as I remember afresh that he has died, high voltage burning over and over. Never less hurtful for the retelling, in these raw days.

There is a longing for it to be different. A desperate longing for him to be there, to help us through this fiend-filled purgatory. He would know just what to say, to ease our torment through this abhorrent anomaly of life. This painful, incongruous existence without him drives endless longing.

I have visions of the events as they might have played out; replay old conversations; wonder repeatedly what we could have missed, whirring it over again and again.

Mostly though it is just a lead-grey insulated numbness. It overwhelms; I think to protect the brain from the distress. I am disengaged from everything else.

I ring work to say I am going to be off – in the first few days I don't think I could ever return. I don't have any guilt about Matt specifically, though my grief soon re-works itself into guilt about not being at work. I think naïvely that two weeks would be plenty.

Two weeks come and go, and I am still unable to manage more than boiling the kettle, only for it to go cold again. All my thoughts and any conversation are totally dominated by what has happened. Other discussion passes me by completely, simply through my own disassociation, washes over me. I trust that Elise will sort me out, and she does. I sit at home, watching TV – a wholeheartedly passive existence. Disconnected.

Of course, she is sharply affected too: she is in the second layer of the onion skin. Many other layers exist, too, her parents in the next layer for example, each tightly bound to the next, separated only by a white diaphanous allium silk.

Andrew, Elise, and I walk round the field. Walking is relatively easy, I can get into a rhythm and avoid conversation, which is impossible anyway. I keep my head down against the melancholy drizzle. The smell of moist air barely registers, unimportant, the dampness on my face the norm.

As we get round to the back of the village, the church and its cemetery looms into focus from another aspect. An unavoidable glance reveals the horror of the day that has changed everything. The scratch marks left by his body and the visible slide-path down the roof engraved onto the tiles. This indelible image carves itself into our brains in painfully slow, clanking blows of the gravestone chisel.

We hug, silently feeling each other's devastation, renewed and fresh. All three a perfect synapse.

Twelve

Matt sat with Rosa, my eldest, in a little informal educational meeting. A mentoring session. With no children of his own, he adored his senior niece.

"Will you teach me about how to edit a video? I need to do one for school."

And with the seriousness of an important job being one to do properly, he took her through the stages of what she'd need.

It was lovely adult time. Rosa switched on, involved, and absorbing. More learning his craft of wit, puns, and banter, than how to mash together a video. This was no matter, this time was precious; it is how families pass on their secrets. How relationships are made strong.

Matt was in his element. It did get technical, however, and he started unwittingly going over her head. "This next bit is called 'In-line editing···'"

I could see her glazing over and he saw it too, then burst out laughing. "I'm really boring, aren't I···!"

He swiftly got back her engagement – an alchemy with atmosphere he'd always had. A gilded ability to make people feel engrossed, intimate, gold-plated within his aura. What a wonderful place it was.

Thirteen

The daily routine: I wake painfully, wondering why he's died, silently bid the children goodbye for school. I might be able to make tea. I sit on the computer looking at things, I'm not sure what. I'm fed tasteless lunch, carefully, lovingly, deliciously prepared by my wife.

After a week off herself, Elise goes back to work. I eat tasteless lunch, uncarefully, angrily, distractedly prepared by myself. I silently say hello to the children as they come home from school, then flop sadly on the sofa in the gloom, watching whatever is flickering in front of me until I mope mutely, early to bed. I am lovingly kissed by my family before restless sleep.

I ring those that need to know, my uncles, aunts, his bank, his mortgage company. Moments of rare courage in the first few days, and my brain steps up to it. I cry down the phone, though hold it together enough to explain disjointedly for a few minutes what has happened.

The ripples of grim news spread rapidly; how widely this violent blow has landed. These little paper boats we float about in, so easily overturned by the waves. How many people are affected by this unexpected horror?

I go up and back many times to Salisbury on the train as we plan the funeral. The first time I arrive back to Bristol I walk back from the station in the cutting January wind. I turn distractedly into a pub I've never been to, sit on the stool and drink a pint. I don't want to go home to face more conversation. I am too drained, too exhausted with the whole thing.

I watch our family Christmas videos on my phone as I sit there alone in The Phoenix, an odd, briefly joyous yet simultaneously intensely unhappy moment unfolds: Matt dancing on the tennis court with Henry, both so alive just a few days ago. HOW CAN HE BE DEAD?

Tears stream, the afternoon drinking clientele aloof, mildly bewildered at my distress I expect, though no one says anything. The lonely privacy of city life. Never judge anyone's emotions – who knows what they've been through?

We plan the funeral, we open cards of condolence, we talk and talk. We sit in silence, in stunned silence. Cry, lots of tears.

My GP signs me off.

The routine brightens over the weeks - six or eight in total - that I am off work. I start going for walks, long ones with the dog, my brain my rather unwelcome companion, it is lumbering-slow, critical, dull.

I get a call from one of my colleagues in the weeks before the funeral. We go out, my first trip away from the dry-retching routine. A simple, unmemorable drink in many ways. She asks how I am, how we are. Cares about me and asks how long I might be off for. Oh, probably back next week, I say, I think I can cope.

I am off for another month; I just have no insight.

Over time however, I do settle. That month passes; the funeral comes and goes. I get extensions on my sick note, despite my guilt about leaving work in the lurch, having to cope with my absence. All that work seemingly so important at the time, yet instantly I dropped it; proving how droppable it all actually was. It is picked up and absorbed by someone else without my knowledge, loving remote support.

How little our daily grinds mean in the long run and how much, instead, these tiny kindnesses matter when the chips are down.

The winter flowering cherry comes into blossom, tiny soft pink bursts of gentle reassurance.

Fourteen

A big family has its benefits. Plenty of people to play football with; always someone who sees your point of view (though you must search amongst others who invariably do not); always someone who will listen, to encourage, to be there. A source of reliable comrades, planted solidly on blood-infused bedrock, always on hand.

Yet when I need them most, to be understood by someone who's been there all my life, it turns out my wonderful family cannot respond. Buried individually in their own pitch-black hell, woefully supportive, through no fault of their own.

Seeing tears and stinging agony in them triggers me as much as my own suffering. Seeing it echoed in those I love most a huge part of the trauma.

Fifteen

"The police are coming tomorrow night, just for a chat",
Dad announces.

They arrive in a pair, a man and a woman. Detectives.
Detectives? What are detectives needed for?

We wonder anxiously.

In the event it was fine; they are kind, willing us to tell
them news, snippets of information. No politician certainty
required, no erudite explanation, no six o'clock headlines
of clarity - which is lucky, because we are still so jumbled,
confused, real.

We meet around the dining table, still scattered with
Matt's things, the funeral planning sheets, the now
redundant, feckless Christmas cards. Pointless ephemeral
glitter, now the world has changed.

We have his computer there - we've been interrogating it for clues as to what had been going on. His journal is chaotic, more a list of ideas, thoughts, dreams, and fears. Rambling yet strangely organised, it is just as Matt would have written a diary. It is a swirl of wonder and uncertainty in equal measure, the caldron from which his next life projects would be summoned.

Yet, it is so difficult to explain to them, in this overwhelming grief-induced brain-fog, what has happened. The vapours too viscous to see through.

"What was his state of mind in the days before he died?"

"His state of mind⋯? I don't know. Well, it was fine, I mean normal, I mean he was up and down, I mean he had his melancholy moments, you know?"

How hard it is to encapsulate what we all know so well. His emotional variability, his bright, his shade, his character. Capturing his essence is absolutely key to explaining his potential state of mind. This is harder than it seems.

He was complex, introverted yet outgoing. Fun yet at times tormented. Aren't we all, to some degree? He was an eye catching rogue sweet pea in the hedgerow green. Enticing.

Yes, he had been sending texts in the very middle of the night. Happy ones, in truth: to my parents-in-law. I have no idea why. Why was he up all night? Who knows? That was just Matt, being Matt, predictably unpredictable. That bit wasn't too much of a surprise.

Yes, Chris wrestling tiredly with an early-rising baby had met him at five a.m. on the morning he died, wandering around the kitchen in his slippers, the ones he climbed the damp church tower steps in, but he was cheerful. "I'm just going off to watch Blue Planet!"

Chris is at a loss; shattered by the idea that he was the last to see him alive. Could we have done something, prevented the tragedy? Who knows? If only we had understood his state of mind. It was hard enough to figure out when he was with us, let alone after he'd died so unexpectedly.

"So can you explain the verger's staff, found on top of the church tower from where he fell?"

I am stunned. "Er, what?" This is odd news to us. A church ornament – a wooden rod a few feet long with a simple metal cross at its tip – that would have been inside the church. He must have picked it up and taken it up the tower.

"No⋯. No idea about that." *What?* Even in his most Matt moment, it was impossible to explain or deduce his tangential thinking.

"Might someone have been up there with him? They could have taken it up?"

And with the police gently probing, and amidst the ambiguity, I drift off and discover a crazy thought with the violent surprise of a sharp knife hidden beneath the washing-up bubbles.

Are they thinking someone killed him?

"Was someone else there? Could anyone else have been involved? What happened that night? Might anyone else have had a motive?"

I look around the table in a fresh hell, testing out this horror-film theory.

Dizzying, repulsive thoughts. My brain has whirred away from reality, set-about and harried, frayed by the desolation of his death. My mourning mind spins me away from truth, reason and common sense. I am tied to the deck in a typhoon, the ship certain to be lost, with the wind howling about me. Lightning bays for blood.

I drag myself back from the irrational edge and look blankly at the Police, who are, after all, just doing their job.

And if I've painted him as up and down and inconsistent, I should show that he was steadier than that. He worked successfully as a TV director, ran his own company, lived in his own flat in London and rented one out in Bristol ("My pension", he called it). He had friends, parties, a next-door neighbour with an Oscar: a mentor whom he treasured and admired. He had godchildren; not that he believed in God. He was busy. He had a trip planned to kite surf in Sri Lanka.

He loved stories, music, gardening, questions, writing, eating, drinking, jokes, jibes, new ideas, not being pigeonholed, making odd noises when he answered the phone, beekeeping, staying up late making merry, meeting people.

He talked to everyone and treated them all the same. Treated them as you would want to be treated. Friendly, interested, passionate, he made acquaintances as easily in the supermarket checkout queue or with the barrister he met on a skiing holiday. He could make you feel like you were the most special human in his world.

So why, then, if he was so capable, so engaging, so charming, would he throw himself off the indifferent church roof to his death in the December chill?

Well, his gloomier side was there undeniably, underlying him: undermining. He had been depressed as a teenager, perhaps triggered by cannabis. This had gone by his twenties, though it left a quarry-lake-deep existentialist questioning, a needle-sharp sense of self-criticism and a powerful mind, wanting to analyse and understand. It was capable of spiralling, worrying and destabilising. He could make you feel unwanted, ignored and rejected when he turned inwards. He would forget or ignore his diary commitments, creating disappointment and annoyance at the careless kick of the realisation that you'd been dropped in the verge.

It could push girlfriends away when they got too close to him, meaning he'd never settled down. It meant he always worried his films were never good enough, his self-doubt could become all-consuming. He needed time on his favourite blue chair in the sitting room, craved his daily drop of introverted introspection, time away from the world.

Yet ultimately, we don't know if this side overtook him at the end. He had seemed in a happy place when we'd seen him. A book arrived by post the day he died, the delivery driver coarsely plonking it, unknowingly, on the doorstep when no-one answered the door. He was going to read about Martin Luther, to get to the bottom of the Reformation, you know. Classic Matt reading. So, who orders a book for the day after their death if they're planning to kill themselves?

"It seems most likely to me," as I think out loud to the police, "that he'd had an unsettled night, drained by lack of sleep, and gone up the tower". (Why go up the tower···?)

My best rationalisation that he looked over the edge, looked over into the all-encompassing darkness, felt surrounded by the shadowy depths of winter and wondered, *What if?* Tottered forwards, stumbling, wondering what the point of life was anyway, *God it can be hard*.

Looked over, just testing, into the flowing inky black, closed his eyes and leant forwards, to see if the cold crisp air would support him.

Sixteen

Henry had got a new street sledge for Christmas, a favourite present from Matt. It was warship-grey hard molded plastic with exhilarating orange wheels, a scooped-out base for sitting. Well, lying was best, actually: get aerodynamically flat, fast, hold the handles tight.

Matt had got his camera out, lured by a rare golden hour on a mild December afternoon. In fact, the whole family was tempted. TV too stale on a rare jewel of a day. The damp, soft, tangy smell of fallen leaves aroused by the clement warmth.

We looked on as Henry had first go. The old shiny red motorbike helmet, with its leatherette trim, had been pulled dustily from the back of the cupboard. I remember rescuing it many years ago from the grubby reeds by Harnham Mill, washing it, polishing it back to dressing-up-box glory. Its main job psychologically cosmetic rather than true physical protection, you suspect.

Groups had formed around each activity. Henry drew focused support staff for his first run. Gauging the corner, the steepness of the hill. Talking about racing lines. I talked about watching out for cars, in a fatherly way. Of course, Boxing Day traffic was hardly a concern, and we relaxed into the thrill of the rides.

Matt had got it into his mind to make a little video. He was interviewing people in his inimitable style. Asking perceptive and often difficult questions, he then tittered from behind the shelter of the camera. He softened and encouraged and teased. We all tried to play up to him, wanted failingly to match his wit and spark.

And with a cry that he was ready, we focused on the action. Henry pushed off, and rolled, and rolled faster down the road, picking up pace. Heads flicked between us···it looked fun! Now, of course, filled with confidence having nailed his first ride, he showed characteristic nonchalant pride in having done so, as he pulled the sledge back up the slope, chest puffed out.

The helmet was passed to me. My middle age sensibilities suggested I start a little further down the hill, to reduce the speed and angle round the corner. Family jeers pushed me back to the top. I slid myself onto the sledge, heart palpitating, blood-rushing at my ears and set off.

The soles of my shoes were flat and scrabbled noisily on the slippery wet tarmac. Steering with subtle movements of my weight, I gathered speed, swiftly approached the corner, wow it was visceral, and low, and on the limit. *Am I going to make the corner? Don't panic!* I controlled it, leant, pressed, hoped! The apex approached and I was rocketing past Matt who rapidly rotated to follow me with his lens. Tears streamed, the wind in my eyes. IT WAS SO QUICK! Then the hill faded and the speed diminished, thank goodness, I'd done it. That was GREAT!

I leapt up, triumphantly punching the air in celebration of the non-catastrophe that I'd claimed. Jubilantly pulled at the helmet buckle, ready to pass on the baton.

Matt was next, and I received instructions to video. He gave me a crash course in his complex, manually focused camera. I doubted that I was going to be up to it, though he didn't mind.

He bulleted past, you could see the grimace of joy on his face as he went through at top speed. Red helmet attached, to prove the danger.

Suddenly he was down, high-fiving Elise who was on backstop duty. She'd gone down there to avoid having to have a go, instead to be safety marshal - a post plainly too important to relinquish.

We were universally animated by the zip of successive rides, it didn't diminish with experience.

Matt filmed everything, changed angles, lenses, creative ideas. Restricted only by the premature mid-afternoon dusk, the fading honeyed sunshine filtering through the bare branches, that sent us home for tea and left-over Christmas cake. The perfect afternoon.

Seventeen

The coroner must be involved, of course, the cause being sudden death by accident or suicide; either qualified. Their job to review the facts and decide on the balance of probability what has happened.

It is slow, delayed by the police not being able to unlock Matt's phone. We rack our brains for the code: no, it isn't the same "household password", easily guessed by those in the know, and long deemed a family joke⋯ we are still surprised when it doesn't work.

No matter what we suggest, it is locked, and locked for good.

Mum is overwhelmed by what no mother should ever face. She wants proof by way of the photos that will surely be found on the phone, that he must have been up the tower on some creative mission. Albeit a crazily ill-conceived, insomniac, pre-dawn photographic expedition.

She keeps pointing out that he'd slipped off the tower to the East, by way of proving that he must have been purposefully facing the dawn when he slipped and fell, a tragic accident.

It makes me irritated that she is latching onto this, I don't know why. Maybe because it contradicts my own best tacit elucidation of what has happened, crystalized over a winter of relentless soul-searching. There is an uncomfortable realisation that each of us now hold our own divergent narratives, despite the same sickening opening scene.

By now, several months have passed and I am back at work on the day of the hearing. I have Elise in my place, being our family representative at the coroner's court, at the formal review of the police's evidence to determine the truth.

Historically the coroner would do their best to collude with family wishes to record accidents instead of suicide, were the circumstances not clear cut. To avoid the stigma. To avoid more guilt, perhaps.

This does resonate, to a degree. If he were in sound mind then we can blame him for being an idiot, for putting himself in his own mortal danger. But that this would be his own failing: one we can perhaps forgive him of, in time.

If, on the other hand, he was so racked by brooding demons, driving him dervishly to jump, then perhaps we will inherit another layer of culpability upon the many others that have surfaced after his death, that we could have said or done something to soothe the suicidal feelings. No one wants a dead brother on their conscience.

Yet for me, I am content that he'd not been suicidal, though could still have killed himself. I have come to accept that a semi-accidental suicide can be a thing. I have never had cause to think of the various gruesome permutations of intent during self-ending before, yet now want to methodically understand all the grim possibilities, no matter how unpleasant.

Ultimately, as a GP, I talk to people with suicidal feelings all the time. However, despite our best efforts, some people's most intimate thoughts are not within our gift to control nor ameliorate, no matter how hard we try. I am always fighting the corner for my patients, to normalise mental illness, to attempt to reduce its stigma, so perhaps an acceptance of the ultimate expression of suicidal feeling as a deeply personal matter is something I can bear.

I can now grasp and feel comfortable living with the fact that Matt might have killed himself, as a fact, even if as a feeling, it still wrenches me in two.

As the coroner's court convenes, new evidence is submitted from the drone that had gone to survey the scene. It had been far too slippery on the roof, with only a small low parapet wall surrounding the tower, to send officers up in person. An electronic police eagle was sent up to spy.

They conclude that the freshly loosened tiles on the inside of the tower roof prove that he had been facing inwards, not outwards as my plot line had demanded. The coroner concludes clear accident.

As I hear this back from Elise, I am re-stunned into the zombified silence that I'd adopted for much of the first few months, after my own story - which had been slowly, logically, and carefully crafted - has been put up for inspection, challenged, waved dismissively away and destroyed. I am unable to speak again, my numb brain rotten-apple soft.

This is a violent jolt, a blow from the hammer that shatters my sheen of resilience. I can smell the burning polish. That veneer of recovery knocked so easily away.

Eighteen

The funeral, in three parts.

Joy

Once the immediate, icy grip of shock has dissipated, we set to the funeral. It is important. How to show what he means to us, to demonstrate our love and loss?

How to honour him, to preserve him, to quickly save as much of him as we can? We are scooping up waning memories like a child grasping at spilt sweets on the counter, liable to roll away and be gone forever. We have lost something we should have put more carefully away.

We sit at the kitchen table and plan. Walk round the field and plan. Endless planning: to make it perfect. Support comes from every angle, as we are gathered up to the collective warm bosom of those who treasure us, it is a huge, worthwhile communal effort. This is the task that draws us out of our dazed immobility.

Given we had six weeks to do it, it comes off as a huge achievement; certainly, a rather grim-faced and wholly unwanted event, though successful, nonetheless.

The village too swings into powerful action – sorting out parking, tractors pulling trailers of guests from the distant fields into the vicinity of the church, whose car parking for five is clearly going to be inadequate. Someone rings the council to get the road double salted, freezing February ice is forecast. They oblige with a gritter alongside a grimy yellow snow plough, beacon flashing. A proper seasonal cortège.

We hire a small awning next to the church, so everyone can be held close to the service. We'll have hundreds, we predict, pews will be at a premium.

Catering, done at cost by a sympathetic neighbour who works in the industry. Flowers are ordered from the local flower shop in Tisbury, another family friend.

A second, main marquee is put on the rec, where we played football as kids. It is all where it needs to be.

There is so much to be done:

Andrew, a draughtsman by trade, draws a map of the village to direct.

An old flat mate of Matt's, an artist, helps design the

marquee's interior decorations.

The village patriarch coordinates the local response – a point of contact, a safe space to control logistical questions brought nervously to a grieving family.

I buy some old pine doors to pin photographs to; we had piles of them to mount.

Elise loves me, and us all.

She picks teasels tearfully and weaves leafless willow branches around the marquee's bare poles.

Adam coordinates the elegant funeral service, mainly a celebration of photos, quotes, and music he loved.

Chris supports Mum, too broken hearted to do much more than just be there, a very reasonable position. A family mainstay.

Claire arranges an email address to collect electronic eulogy. Printed quotes are collated and smartly tied up to the willow, soft downy buds at the branch tips.

Dad is the central stalwart of the whole operation; he seems oddly detached from the sadness at times. Taking time to come to terms with it, we sense, being practical preferable to being punctured.

Our immediate family, wives, girlfriend and boyfriend love us all, and don't step back from the crisis. They, our individual lifeboats; our inner-secret confidants; our soul-saviours.

Countless others do countless other things to keep the show on the road, the highest quality community oil.

Flowers are spread around, simple spring blooms, snowdrops, pansies, early daffodils. Matt would have loved it being seasonal, local, and real.

The children float about like helium balloons above the grief, bringing mundane normality as a reminder of the future. Them being there proves the cycle of life, that we all must leave space when we go, for others to step into.

We are setting up his favourite things on the church altar.

Things he hadn't finished using:

A picture of a beehive – he had loved pollinating Peckham.

His Bafta nomination certificate – he loved giggling about how he'd met Naomi Campbell at the awards ceremony which more than made up for not winning, even if it turned him to a jibbering wreck.

His kitesurfing board, his passion.

And a small plastic toy dog, a gift from his goddaughter, who has loving returned it to him, post-mortem.

Pain

And so, if the funeral is made of pure love, which it is, and if the drive to do it perfectly is important, which it is, why does it have a downside? Well, it brings home some home truths.

Grief is the price of loving. Everyone dies, yet we're foolish and neglectful in our preparations. How are we so naïve in our love that we think it endless? Why do we assume that adoration is without debt? It must be paid, a devil's pact.

Grief drives desire and longing. There is so much missing to be done. And oh! how I miss him.

How many things I wish to say to him? How many little things I want him to see, to bear witness to? To join in with, to reminisce over. I see a poster for a show and want to go with him, want to be in his company as we jaunt round the museum, tittering at other people doing normal people-like things. A favourite Matt pastime.

I want him to see my children grow up, I want to see his children, though he had none, grow up. I invent little stories about what he'd be doing now, where he'd be. I imagine him cycling round Peckham, like in that photo we've got, chatting up girls on a night out. I send him on trips to Sri Lanka, to kite surfing holidays with his friends. There is the frangipani tree to visit, planted for him on the beach in memoriam, its fragrant scent drifting over the surf.

We meet the day before the funeral, for the formal interment. Just ten of us, in the church, setting up for the formal service the next day. The same vicar, who I've not yet forgiven, presiding. I hold my tongue, knowing it is me, not her.

It is a sub-zero, drab, whipping-wind kind of day. Snow is anticipated though not yet here. We huddle, our hearts like heavy wet woollen coats. Bitterly pulled down.

We stand sullenly around the frozen mud, where someone has dug a shallow hole for the ashes. I hadn't wanted to go to the crematorium. Too crushing, too formulaic, too unlike Matt. He would have hated that. In the end, a private pouring of his ashes into the ground is still dismal enough, so hard to decant away all that memory. How dismal, to have to pour your brother into the ground.

As it happens, the wind catches the ashes as we tip, spiriting part of him up into the air – he would have loved the jeopardy, the sacrilegious, unorthodox ending. He would have been silently laughing in the back row at the horror of the unceremonious, unscripted departure from the solemn sanctity of the task. Watching, it would be

Matt, always observing how other's reacted, who would have enjoyed the spectacle, the more peril the better.

Rosa says she has got some on the sleeve of her coat. It somehow feels right, if rather unhallowed. Clear that Matt wants to fly away, yearning for more adventure, defying the missed opportunity.

We re-turf the top of the grave, the job complete. The uncaring wind continues irreverently, weighty and unabated. Yet at that moment, the blue sky glimpses, visible despite the best intentions of the hulking pregnant clouds.

Joy

The promised snow arrives vehemently overnight; then the vengeful sky dissipates.

The curtains hide a crisp, clear, bright, azure, shining, glinting, silent, soft-white snowy wonderland. The day of the funeral promises to be grimly sparkling.

We go to the marquee to do the final prep, to find the owners had been out in the night, to shovel the snow from the roof and turn the heaters on. Final proof, if any were needed, of so much hidden help.

All of us tense with expectation. Dressed up smartly, it feels oddly like a Christmas morning, there is a rising anticipation.

When the time comes to formally stand at the lych gate, to greet the wave of mourners, we are washed in pride and tearful joy – so many people have come. Wave after wave of those to hug, to console, to be consoled. It is a tsunami of love, sent from all over the world. From every corner of Matt's history – some lifelong known to us, some never previously met.

We'd sent an open invite – in the end nearly five hundred come. Squeezing themselves into the church then overflowing to stand outside, speakers set up to beam the service. Those outside gravely revel in the snow, the atmosphere, and the wonder of the day.

Matt would have loved the paradoxical reactions of people as they mixed feelings of intrinsic delight at the quality of the day juxtaposed with the inherent grief of the occasion and the formal rites and its detached ceremonial process.

After the memorial service, we march down the hill to the marquee. Now flooded with food, drink and all those glorious people, it is resplendent in dark funereal magic, just as it should be. The room strengthens and buzzes with the collective power of people united in a vital common purpose.

We agree that we'll all take our turns in speaking. I take the lead, telling tearful stories of Matt, how my first memory of him was of hitting him so firmly with that stone on the sandy hillside path.

Adam, promoted, now incongruously and unwantedly to number two, reads a heartfelt, funny eulogy.

Chris does the same, remembering the same man yet from another angle, another loving perspective, beautifully picking out his uniqueness.

Claire reads a poem, witty, reminiscent, powerful – all those wonderful little things that make a person, remembered. It's about things that he had taught her over his life, entitled, "How to flare your nostrils".

Of course, Matt being from a TV background we need to have video. His work friends deliver this with a crisply edited reel of his life, poignantly starting with cinefilm snapshots of him growing up, then to his work as a director, ending in him explaining in an interview about how he approached making documentaries. Hearing his booming voice on the loudspeaker at his own funeral is intense and overwhelming, seeing him talking to us again is too much to bear.

It does feels good, too, if good can be felt six weeks after your brother dies. It makes me think how much he would have enjoyed his own wake. Five hundred people who have been touched by him, who feel the need to be there, who've made the effort to come through the snow, through the winter, through their grief. He would have been amazed. Old school friends, people he'd been on holiday with, TV mentees and mentors, those he worked with, those he admired and valued, all come to pay their respects.

All come to celebrate his life with us. Come to share it, and to show us how profoundly he is loved and missed, absent, now, where he still should be.

What more can we want?

And after the formal, comes the chatting, the buzz, the circulating. The recurring theme, how much he made each individual feel like they were the centre of his world. An uncanny gift, for he meant it too. This was no con-trick. The best of his impassioned, engaged, fun-loving character shines from every reminiscence.

We stay there for the rest of the day, guests drift away slowly and reluctantly, leaving the closest friends and family, then just the immediate.

We sit around the table of pork pies and cask ale, from The Horseshoe of course, and celebrate the glory of a day gone to plan, layered on the unnerving background horror of what shouldn't have had to be.

Nineteen

The funeral draws a line, a public recognition of the loss and the trauma and the heartache. Not specifically cathartic now, more necessary process, it is evidently an integral part of the healing and us moving on.

Flawless February sunshine and polished snow meet us the following day. It is obvious that we should make the most of it. Matt would have wanted us to get out in it, we decided. The kids want to too, visibly overjoyed that we had finally found some hidden energy for normality. Mourning can be put to one side for a day.

We shoot down the hill on the sledge that has been dredged up from the cellar. Tobogganing recklessness down the hill, a mild salve, a little sweet-smelling emollient for our dry grief.

Twenty

Two weeks after the funeral, I go back to work. Initially, my lack of insight had surprised me though now I simply accept it. I trust others to see that I was ok. Ask, and let them help.

Work has silently and simply swept up the loose ends, coping immediately, sending flowers, promising whatever time off was required. They care. It takes the pressure off what is plainly going to be needed, a few months off and a graded return.

I am tuned-in to hearing grief, nodding in wary acknowledgement as it passes. People I know have since lost friends, relatives, children. Each lost relationship unique and special. There is no normal for grief, it is entirely singular in its own way.

It's true that the heartache is the same, though the way it grows, flows, fades and scars is for that person alone to witness. Supporting them is an act of human love, of patience, of understanding. Careful listening to the testimony of their experience is key.

Time, as the platitude says, is a healer - though it is certainly tortoise not hare, it will not be rushed.

So I go back to the surgery, under the mantra of that other great platitude, one-day-at-a-time. I have reduced commitments, no additional management responsibilities, shortened surgeries. Work eases me back in, keeping a careful weather-eye on me; popping in, to see how I was getting on.

I am a more rounded doctor now; I can more effectively empathise with those who share their grieving burden. My shoulders broader, to better help them carry their load.

Twenty-One

Matt loved taking pictures. Loved the magic of photography and its power to convey. He was always on hand to share the mysteries of light and how to capture it. His passion to film, to tell stories, to enlighten. Photos do that in an instant. Histories conjured up in a second; a glance to tell those thousand words.

We collect as many as we can before the funeral, hundreds and hundreds, we print out the best for a huge demonstration of connected life. Digital pictures display on an endless slideshow on the screen all afternoon, we have so many they don't repeat.

They tell tales of adventure, of spirit, of so many wonderful experiences, shared with so many fabulous people. They show how the world has joy to give if we seek it and that life should be lived in all its abundance. It tells a story of a life to be celebrated and to recognise how much he'd enjoyed his forty years on this bonkers planet.

Of course, I think he would have wanted to go on. To continue bringing joy, random uncertainty, and questioning wit to our lives for another forty years. It is not to be.

And whilst I miss him desperately, he lives on in glorious detail in those pictures created through our collective memory.

Twenty-Two

Whist I load it with anticipation, my first day back holds little drama. I have all past memory for facts, all prior knowledge for how to do it. My doctor's deportment pings back the moment I call the first patient in.

I hadn't really thought about how I'd deal with death or dying for those I care for. How would I cope with the patient for whom I'd got to break the news of a new terminal diagnosis, for example? In the event, it is back to normal with a gentle jolt, like a train smoothly pulling away from the station.

Grief walks through the door on my first day back, too, and reminds me of its desire to do its own thing. A fifty-year-old lady, who's booked herself in to talk about her knee.

"Sorry, I can't think straight," she starts, "I've just heard that my sister died in a car crash last night."

"Oh my God, how horrible for you", I answer, after a pause, hoping the compassion is feeding through my tone of voice. I wait and let the wave of internal emotion judder through me. "Shall we forget about your knee, I'm sure you'll want to talk about your sister?"

"No," she answered diffidently and to my surprise, "It's too new, too raw, and I just want to get my leg looked at, it's been aching for months."

"......?

Are you sure⋯⋯?"

And so, at her request to brush it under the carpet –

denial, I guess – we look at her knee: mildly arthritic. A

few painkillers and some physio, all that's needed to help

her joint.

As she leaves, I remind her that I'll be there to talk more

about her sister, whenever she wants to come back.

She never does.

Every kind of grief as different as every kind of person.

Twenty-Three

My parents have a candle in the middle of their table; Matty's candle.

It is lit every mealtime without much ceremony, though it is never overlooked, never neglected. It is a little piece of the ritual, their way of coping. It soothes us, helps us all see that he is still with us, still at the heart of the family as we simply get back on with our lives.

Remembered at every family event, with every bite. Every morsel of conversation still shared with him.

We have a natural collective understanding about the candle that transcends any simple transmission of light. His way home is distinctly lit.

Twenty-Four

So, am I back to normal? There is a new reality, perhaps, though I'm noticeably changed forever. A five-leaved clover is now one frond down; still lucky but not nearly as magical as it once was. The welt has healed, though the wound still stiff and immobile.

I accept that this is the new normal, and that I've grown, transformed, learnt to cope with it over time, finally grasping that life and death is the normality.

Three years have now passed, building experience of anniversaries, Christmases, birthdays that, whilst so painful initially, have been tempered by the weathering of time. A bit of counselling went a long way: sleep returned, alcohol lessened, tears dried.

In the interim, Covid has claimed many lives on top of the normal baseline of mortality. I've since heard so many other stories of grief, of tragedy, of aching loss.

Each one reminds me how lucky I am, despite everything.

And still, the worst symptom, going on, are the internal cattle-prods triggered by my unconscious thoughts, "I wonder how Matt is, I haven't heard from him in a while?"

·····································*Oh*

A song he'd like

A film we watched

A pub we sat in twenty years ago

Scampi Fries

A text he'd laugh at

A hilltop walk we did

A silver Golf in the rear-view mirror

A polished art gallery floor to slide on

A photograph he'd critique

An unusual bird he'd be interested in

A joke he'd roar at

A holiday he'd love to join

Every little thing he used to say.

Acknowledgments

Thank you, cherished family and friends. Your support, love, wisdom and strength have seen me through.

Specifically, I'm deeply indebted to Ben Fergusson the word tsar, and Andy Fergusson who designed the wonderful cover. I'm so grateful for all those first-readers, who encouraged me to get this far; and to the Cordells, who saved me from a multitude of errors.

Tom Pelly is a GP in Bristol, having been a doctor for twenty years. This is his first publication.

Cover design: based on a photo of Matt Pelly's silhouette, taken on a family walk from Wake House on Christmas Day, 2014

Printed in Great Britain
by Amazon

57557159R10066